Helping Your Child to Read

Annemarie Young

OXFORD
UNIVERSITY PRESS

OXFORD
UNIVERSITY PRESS

Great Clarendon Street, Oxford, OX2 6DP, United Kingdom

Oxford University Press is a department of the University
of Oxford. It furthers the University's objective of excellence
in research, scholarship, and education by publishing worldwide.
Oxford is a registered trade mark of Oxford University Press
in the UK and in certain other countries

First published 2018

British Library Cataloguing in Publication Data
Data available

ISBN: 978-0-19-276440-9

10 9 8 7 6 5 4 3 2 1

Paper used in the production of this book is a natural, recyclable
product made from wood grown in sustainable forests. The
manufacturing process conforms to the environmental
regulations of the country of origin.

Printed in China

Acknowledgements

With thanks to Kate Ruttle

Cover illustrations by: Korky Paul, Alex Brychta, Deborah Allwright

Illustrations by: Alex Brychta, Korky Paul, Judy Brown, Kate Slater,
Sue Mason, Andrés Martínez Ricci, Martin Chatterton

Photographs: **p9**, **p10**: Shutterstock

Contents

The Read with Oxford Stages

To help you choose the right book for your child, you can use the **Read** with **Oxford Stages** – a simple levelling system to help you navigate your child's reading journey from their first steps in phonics and learning to read, all the way to reading independently. The six colour-coded **Stages** use descriptions to help you accurately gauge your child's reading level. These **Stages** are also aligned with Oxford Levels and Book Bands (used by schools) so that you can match the **Read** with **Oxford** books to those your child brings home from school. Approximate ages are provided, but remember that every child learns to read at their own pace. Using the **Read** with **Oxford Stages** will ensure that your child is reading books at the right level for them.

	Equivalent Oxford Levels	Book Bands best fit	Approximate age range
STAGE 1 First steps: I am starting to use letter sounds to read simple words			
	1 and 1+	Lilac & Pink	3 – 4
STAGE 2 Early reader: I can use letter sounds to read simple words and short sentences			
	2 and 3	Red & Yellow	4 – 5
STAGE 3 Growing reader: I am starting to read more words and longer sentences with less help			
	4 and 5	Blue & Green	4 – 5
STAGE 4 Gaining confidence: I sometimes read by myself, and I can read lots of everyday words			
	6 and 7	Orange & Turquoise	5 – 6
STAGE 5 Becoming independent: I can read and enjoy a whole story by myself			
	8 and 9	Purple & Gold	6 – 7
STAGE 6 Independent reader: I can read and understand longer chapter books by myself			
	10, 11 and 12	White, Lime & Brown	7 – 8

Learning to read

This book shows you how to start supporting your child from an early age so that learning to read is successful and enjoyable for you both. Children whose parents read with them at home and talk about books have a huge advantage.

Read with **Oxford** includes stories involving well-known characters such as Biff, Chip and Kipper and Winnie and Wilbur. It also offers phonic stories written by Julia Donaldson and collections of phonic traditional tales, as well as longer books with separate chapters to help build reading stamina, and much more. Giving children a broad variety of books to read allows them to develop wider reading interests, and encourages reading for pleasure.

How to make your child a successful reader

From babyhood onwards, you can help your child to enjoy books, to understand how books work, and to learn what it means to be a 'reader'. This book gives you practical tips and ideas for each of the stages of a child's reading development, including playing games, doing activities and reading a wide range of books together.

How can the Read with Oxford books help my child?

The books are designed to support children from their first steps in phonics all the way to reading independence. The range offers a variety of different story genres and styles, including traditional tales, humorous adventures, stories that make you think, laugh and get emotionally involved. There are six **Read** with **Oxford Stages**, providing gradual progression. At the earlier stages, phonics storybooks enable children to read and practise their letters and sounds as they do at school, and stories for wider reading introduce young readers to common words and everyday language. The higher stages provide longer books that offer variety and encourage reading stamina and confidence.

Tips and ideas

The books in **Read** with **Oxford** include practical tips for you, and fun activities for your child, to help them develop their reading skills. Most children enjoy stories, although some prefer information books. There are many excellent information books available for children at all stages of their reading development.

Choosing the right books for your child

The chart on page 4 gives an overview of the **Read with Oxford Stages**, a unique levelling system designed to help you choose which books to share with your child. It is important to note that the age guidance is approximate for all **Stages**. This is particularly true at the start of a child's reading development; some children are ready to start reading as early as age three, while others may not be ready until they are at least four, if not later. Guidance is given on page 10. Every child develops at their own pace. If you are in any doubt, ask your child's teacher for advice.

Stage 1 First steps: I am starting to use letter sounds to read simple words (approximately 3–4-year-olds)

What children can do at Read with Oxford Stage 1:

- Enjoy sharing and discussing books.
- Join in with language play (e.g. songs and nursery rhymes).
- Recognise most or all of the letters of the alphabet and be aware of one simple sound for each letter.
- Read at least a few simple words by sounding out and blending, e.g. *s-a-t, sat* (see page 9).
- Start to recognise a few common tricky words like 'and', 'the' (page 9).
- Talk about a story they have read or listened to.
- Sometimes relate books to their own experience.
- Concentrate for about 5–10 mins.

Stage 2 Early reader: I can use letter sounds to read simple words and short sentences (approximately 4–5-year-olds)

What children can do at Read with Oxford Stage 2:

- Read short sentences and a wider range of simple words by sounding out and blending, e.g. *f-ee-t, feet* (p.9).
- Read some words of more than one syllable.
- Recognise and read on sight several common tricky words (e.g. 'was', 'you').
- Read some long vowel sounds (e.g. 'f**ee**t', 'm**oo**n') and adjacent consonants (e.g. '**cr**ash', '**st**ar').
- Explain their views on a book they have read or listened to, and relate stories to their own experience.
- Usually concentrate for around 10 minutes.

Stage 3 Growing reader: I am starting to read more words and longer sentences with less help (approximately 4–5-year-olds)

What children can do at Read with Oxford Stage 3:

- Recognise and read on sight a larger number of common tricky words.

- Read some words where the same sound is made by different letter patterns, e.g. reading the sound /ai/ in words like *rain, make, day*.

- Often use their phonics knowledge and skills automatically, without support and often without having to sound out the words aloud.

- Sometimes notice their own errors while reading and correct them.

- Understand what they read in more depth, and make simple predictions about what comes next.

- Talk about a book they have read with growing confidence, and express opinions about what they have read.

- Usually able to read a whole Stage 3 book in one sitting.

Stage 4 Gaining confidence: I sometimes read by myself, and I can read lots of everyday words (approximately 5–6-year-olds)

What children can do at Read with Oxford Stage 4:

- Many children will have reached the end of their formal phonics instruction, and can usually apply their phonics knowledge automatically, without sounding out or needing to be prompted.

- Often able to read a wide range of familiar and unfamiliar words.

- Most children can choose whether to read silently or aloud. They can often read aloud with pace and expression, taking punctuation into account.

- Usually notice their own errors while reading, and go back over the text to correct misreadings.

- Recognise and read on sight most common tricky words, like 'where', 'once', 'because'.

- Talk about what they have read with growing confidence and independence.

- Select their own books to read, based on the cover and blurb.

- Usually able to read a whole Stage 4 book in one sitting.

Stage 5 Becoming independent: I can read and enjoy a whole story by myself (approximately 6–7-year-olds)

What children can do at Read with Oxford Stage 5:

- Often read silently and quickly, and apply their phonics knowledge automatically (except for the occasional very unfamiliar word).
- Recognise and read on sight a wide range of common tricky words, e.g. 'beautiful', 'eye'.
- Usually read aloud with reasonable pace and fluency, taking punctuation into account and sometimes using appropriate expression to convey meaning.
- Begin to make fewer errors while reading, and usually notice and correct them.
- Usually able to explain their ideas about a story or information book in some detail, and say why they do or don't like a book.
- Understand that there are different types of fiction and non-fiction books.
- Usually able to read a short Stage 5 book in one sitting or, for longer books, at least one complete chapter.

Stage 6 Independent reader: I can read and understand longer chapter books by myself (approximately 7–8-year-olds)

What children can do at Read with Oxford Stage 6:

- Read silently and quickly most of the time. They can use their knowledge to help them tackle unfamiliar words.
- Know and read automatically a wide range of common tricky words, like 'people', 'friend', 'through'.
- Notice and correct (rare) errors when they do occur.
- Confidently comment on characters, story and plot, and express reasoned opinions about what they read in fiction and non-fiction.
- Sometimes comment on an author's style and use of language, e.g. using short sentences to create excitement.
- Make independent choices about what to read.
- Usually able to read at least two chapters of a Stage 6 book in one sitting, and keen to attempt longer books.

How does your child learn to read at school?

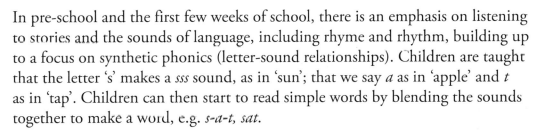

Schools use a range of methods to teach children to read. The main one currently used to start children reading is called 'synthetic phonics'.

In pre-school and the first few weeks of school, there is an emphasis on listening to stories and the sounds of language, including rhyme and rhythm, building up to a focus on synthetic phonics (letter-sound relationships). Children are taught that the letter 's' makes a *sss* sound, as in 'sun'; that we say *a* as in 'apple' and *t* as in 'tap'. Children can then start to read simple words by blending the sounds together to make a word, e.g. *s-a-t, sat*.

After they have learned the more straightforward letter-sound relationships, they are taught the more complex ones, e.g. that the /igh/ sound, as in 'high', can also be written as *tried*, *cry* and **nine**.

Sounds are not taught in alphabetical order, instead they are taught in the order best suited to begin blending sounds together for reading.

You can listen to the sounds on **oxfordowl.co.uk**. Note that some sounds are pronounced differently according to regional accent, so consult your child's teacher for advice if you are unsure.

Tricky words

Many common, everyday words, like 'the' and 'said' don't follow the phonics rules that your child will be learning in school. These words cannot be read by sounding out. They are sometimes called 'tricky' words or 'high-frequency words'. Read these words out to your child and they will soon learn to recognise them by sight. The **Read** with **Oxford** *Biff, Chip and Kipper: Fun with Words* flashcards are a fun and effective way to practise tricky words.

Stage 1 First steps I am starting to use letter sounds to read simple words

Preparing your child for reading

Sharing books and talking about the pictures with your child from an early age (even as a baby) will increase their language skills and develop their understanding of the world. Your child will be learning how books work – that they have a front and a back and pages that turn to tell a story. They may like to hold the book and try to turn the pages themselves.

As they get a bit older, point to each word on the page as you read, to help your child understand how print works – that the marks on the page carry meaning to tell the story. Once they can sustain concentration for five to ten minutes you will be able to help them get ready to start learning to read.

Children need to develop a range of skills, focusing on the meaning of sentences, the shape of a story and on recognising individual words and letter sounds.

You can support them by:
● talking about stories and using story language
● helping them develop an understanding of letter-sound relationships
● helping them to recognise common words by sight.

In pre-school and early in Reception/Primary 1, the emphasis is on listening to stories and the sounds of language, before introducing phonics.

You can help your child with phonics by playing language games with them: teach them songs and nursery rhymes; invent silly rhymes for them to join in with; clap the rhythms of words; help them to think of 'another word that begins with the same sound as …'.

Once your child has started school, they will probably bring books home to practise their skills. But don't stop reading to your child – this experience promotes reading for enjoyment.

Practical tips

Try to make time to read *to* and *with* your child every day. Choose a time when they are not too tired and you are not too busy. Turn off any distractions such as the TV, radio and mobile phones. Keep reading lots of different books to your child, and keep bedtime reading special. Most picture books will be too hard for them to read, and it's good for them just to listen to a story and look at the pictures with you. Once they have started reading simple books at home or at school, you can ask them to read these with you.

Read with Oxford Stage 1: Biff, Chip & Kipper: *Dad's Birthday and Other Stories*

- Before reading a book together, always talk about the title, the blurb and the pictures on the cover. Ask your child what they think the book might be about. As you read, point to the words. Let them join in if they want to.

- Read with expression and try different voices for different characters. Get your child to join in with refrains like *Run, run, as fast as you can* ....

- Talk about the stories when you've finished reading together. Ask questions like: *What did you like best? What colour was Mum wearing?*

- Re-read the story with your child, encouraging them to join in with repeated patterns.

- Give them lots of praise as they read with you.

In these early stages of their reading development, always read a book aloud before you ask your child to read it with you. This gives them the chance to understand the story, and to hear the words and language patterns. Remember, you are not testing your child; knowing what the book is about will help boost their confidence.

Stage 1 Phonics

Developing and practising phonics skills

- Encourage your child to recognise letters and rhymes.

- Sing the alphabet song while pointing to letters on a printed frieze.

- Recite rhymes they know, like *One, two, three, four, five, Once I caught a fish…*, and get them to supply the missing rhyming word.

- Use modelling clay or playdough to make letter shapes.

- Demonstrate blending by saying the sounds *c-a-t* to read *cat*.

- Use magnetic letters on the fridge and sponge letters in the bath to spell your child's name, and other simple words.

- Find sets of words which begin or end with the same sound.

- Say a short word. Can your child tell you the sounds in the word? (e.g. *sat, s-a-t*). Or say the sounds. Can your child tell you the word? (e.g. *f-i-sh, fish*).

- Find pictures in magazines to make sets of 'Words which begin with …' and make an alphabet scrapbook.

- Use the **Read** with **Oxford** *Biff, Chip and Kipper: Alphabet Games* flashcards and *Julia Donaldson's Songbirds: Phonics Games* flashcards to play alphabet and phonics games.

After you have read a book, play word and letter-spotting games like these: *Can you find the word 'and' on this page? How many words can you find on this page that begin with 't'?*

Stage 1 Reading

When reading a story to or with your child, look through the pictures first, so your child can see what the book is about. Next, read the story to your child, placing your finger under each word as you read. Then read the story again and encourage your child to join in. Re-read the story as many times as your child wants – this helps to build their confidence. Talk about the story together when you have finished.

Developing and practising reading skills

- Draw attention to special story language, such as *Once upon a time* ....

- Play alliterative games, like *Annie got an apple, Ben got a bike*, or rhyming games.

- Encourage your child to retell favourite stories to a friend or grandparent.

- Use the pictures as well as the words to help them understand the whole story.

- Take your child to the library and encourage them to make choices about the books they want to read.

- Enjoy teaching them nursery rhymes and action songs. Play 'I spy' on car journeys or listen to audiobooks.

- Read as many books as you can, to and with your child, including retellings of traditional tales and fairy stories, alphabet books and simple information books.

If your child gets stuck on a word, check first if it can be 'sounded out'. If not, try re-reading the sentence without saying the difficult word. The meaning of the rest of the sentence can often help. If they still can't work out the word, just say it for them to repeat and move on with the story.

Some of the sounds and letter patterns practised in Stage 1

/o/ as in dog and /a/ as in cat; /e/ as in hen,
/k/ as in king
/i/ as in tin and win, and /u/ as in tub and mud
/r/ as in ran, /s/ as in mess and bus
/f/ as in puff and fizz
/ck/ as in back

Useful common but tricky words

go no the I to into
he she said was

Phonics activities

- After you have shared a storybook together, you can start to draw attention to the specific words and letters again.
- Point out the first sound of a word and then ask your child to find another word beginning with the same sound or perhaps think of a rhyming word.
- Ask them to find two words that sound the same.
- Use the phonics activity books and the phonics activities in the **Read** with **Oxford** Stage 1 collections (e.g. *Biff, Chip and Kipper: Silly Races and Other Stories*)

STAGE 1
First steps: I am starting to use letter sounds to read simple words

| Approx. 3– 4 years | Oxford Levels 1 and 1+ | Book Bands Lilac and Pink |

Stage 2 **Early reader** I can use letter sounds to read simple words and short sentences

At this stage your child will be able to read very simple stories, and will be developing their reading skills and strategies. It's as important as ever to keep a good balance between sharing books together for enjoyment and practising early reading skills.

Practical tips

- Keep bedtime reading special. Read lots of new and different books to your child as well as continuing to re-read old favourites.

- Before reading a book together, talk through the story without reading it aloud. Point out any words you think might be difficult and read them out.

- Share the story together, inviting your child to join in on some pages. Give lots of praise as your child reads with you, and help them when necessary.

- Encourage your child to read with expression when re-reading the story.

- Talk about the stories when you've finished reading together. Ask questions like: *What was your favourite bit?*

- Introduce paired reading for some books, where you and your child read from the book at the same time. Pace your reading to the speed of your child. If they struggle with a word, say it clearly for them, then continue reading together. To help them understand the story, ask them what they think might happen next.

Read with Oxford Stage 2: Julia Donaldson's Songbirds: *The Trunk and The Skunk and Other Stories*

I can pick things up.

I can lift things.

28

29

15

Stage 2 **Phonics**

Point out letters that go together, for example, *th*, *sh*, and chunks of words, such as *-ing*. Help your child to recognise these letter patterns and the sounds they make.

Build a word using magnetic letters and ask your child to make a word that rhymes with it, or has one letter that is different, or begins or ends with the same letter.

When your child is reading, help them to look out for whole letter patterns rather than individual letter sounds (e.g. *sh-ee-p* rather than *s-h-e-e-p)*. Write out words they get stuck on, using a different colour for the tricky letter patterns.

Play 'I spy', using words that begin with two consonants, for example, *br, cl, dr, st*; words that end with two consonants, for example, *nd, st, lk*; or words that rhyme.

All the **Read** with **Oxford** collections at Stage 2 contain stories that focus on phonics, introduce particular letter patterns and help children to practise them. The books include tips explaining what to do.

You can also ask your child to look at particular letter patterns in other **Read** with **Oxford** stories, but only do this after they have finished reading and talking about the story.

And don't forget to give your child lots of praise as they read, and when they find letter patterns.

Stage 2 **Reading**

Practising reading skills

Before you start reading, talk about the
title and the picture on the cover. Ask:
What do you think the story is about? Read
the story together, pointing to each word
and inviting your child to join in. Give
lots of praise as your child reads with you,
and help them when necessary.

Clapping out syllables in words and names can help with reading longer
words, e.g. *di-no-saur, choc-o-late*. Point out that some words are made up of
two smaller words, e.g. 'wind' and 'mill' together make windmill.

If your child gets stuck on a word, try their phonics skills first. If it can't be
sounded out, try re-reading the sentence without saying the difficult word.
The meaning of the rest of the sentence can often help. If your child still can't
work out the word, say it for them to repeat, and move on with the story. You
could look at the word more carefully after you have finished reading.

Draw your child's attention to speech marks, punctuation, sound effects and
action words (for example, *BUMP! WHOOSH! CRASH!*).

If your child is still reading 'one-word-at-a-time', let them listen to you reading
fluently and with expression and ask them to copy what you do.

WHOOSH! Flames came
out of the dragon's mouth.

Floppy hid, but the
dragon saw him.

Read with Oxford Stage 2:
Biff, Chip & Kipper: *Wet Feet
and Other Stories*

17

/**v**/ as in Viv; /**x**/ as in fix; /**ch**/ as in Chip; /**oo**/ as in too

/**qu**/ as in quick

/**sh**/ as in shop; /**th**/ as in them

/**ng**/ as in missing

/**ee**/ as in feet

/**sh**/ as in fish

/**oa**/ as in coat

/**ai**/ as in rain

/**oi**/ as in coin

Useful common but tricky words

have like said come some
she was are you they all he

STAGE 2
Early reader: I can use letter sounds to
read simple words and short sentences

Approx. 4–5 years	Oxford Levels 2 and 3	Book Bands Red and Yellow

Stage 3 Growing reader I am starting to read more words and longer sentences with less help

Your child will be building on their earlier reading skills and becoming more confident in their reading. They can often use their knowledge of phonics automatically. The books in the **Read** with **Oxford** series are carefully levelled and the Stage 3 books will be at the right level for your child. The stories are often full of humour, drama and adventure, with a satisfying ending, to keep your child motivated to read while further developing their confidence and their reading skills.

Practical tips

- Don't stop sharing bedtime stories or information books with your child, even if they like to read simple books on their own. Find out what sort of books your child prefers. Choose books together and enjoy talking about them.

- Try sharing a book together, especially if they are finding it challenging – you read one page and your child reads the next. You are showing them what fluent reading sounds like, and if they lose the meaning of the story while concentrating on reading their pages, they can pick up the meaning again while you are reading.

- Try reading slightly more difficult books to your child. Hearing you read fluently will motivate them to want to read fluently themselves.

- Talk about the books you read together. Let them tell you if they don't like a book, and why. It's OK not to like some books.

- Get your child to make links between their own experience and how a character responds in a story.

- As well as reading books aloud together, encourage your child to read silently and independently, especially when they are re-reading favourite books.

Stage 3 Phonics

Practising phonics skills

Make jumbled words. For example, cut out letters from a word like 'night' or 'coat' and ask your child to rebuild the word.

Ask your child to point out words that have the same sound but are written differently, like the /igh/ sound as in *tried, **night**, cry* and ***nine***.

Ask your child to find words that look like they should rhyme but don't, e.g. 'home' and 'come'; 'do' and 'no'. Then ask them to find words which do rhyme even though they look different, e.g. 'come' and 'sum'; 'there' and 'bear'.

Turn the search into a game by timing them, or seeing how many words they can think of to go in each category. This will help your child become familiar with the alternative spellings for sounds and speed up their reading, making it more enjoyable.

All the **Read** with **Oxford** collections at Stage 3 contain stories that focus on phonics, introduce particular letter patterns and help children to practise them. The books include tips explaining what to do.

You can ask your child to look at particular letter patterns in other stories, but only do this after they have finished reading and talking about the story.

And don't forget to give your child lots of praise as they read, and when they find words that contain the new letter patterns.

Read with Oxford Stage 3:
Julia Donaldson's Songbirds:
Tim's Bad Mood and Other Stories

Stage 3 Reading

Practising reading skills

Before you start reading a story, talk about the title and the picture on the cover. Ask: *What do you think the story is about?*

Read the story together, inviting your child to read as much of it as they can. Give your child lots of praise as they read, and help them when necessary.

When your child is reading new words, encourage them to recognise familiar letter patterns in the word and blend them together, for example, *ch-ur-ch, church.*

If they get stuck on a word that isn't a tricky word, encourage your child to say the sounds and blend them together to read the word. If it is a tricky word or they are still having trouble with it, read the word for them and then read the whole sentence again. Focus on the meaning of what they are reading.

When your child re-reads a story ask them to read it with lots of expression. Get them to use different voices for the different characters.

Talk about the stories you read together, asking your child to tell you about it, what they liked – or didn't like. Ask them if they can relate anything in the story to their own life. For example, if the story is about sport or a hobby, ask them why they think it's good to have a sport or a hobby.

Read with Oxford Stage 3:
The Moon in the Pond and Other Tales

Some of the sounds and letter patterns practised in Stage 3

/**ee**/ as in beach and cheese
/**igh**/ as in tried, night, cry and nine
/**ai**/ as in Craig, day, game
/**f**/ as in dolphin
/**oa**/ as in coat, stove, Joe, snow, ago
/**n**/ as in knight, not
/**oo**/ as in flew and glue
/**s**/ as in dress, nurse, palace and city
/**oo**/ as in wood, pudding and could
/**le**/ as in uncle
/**ow**/ as in down and out
/**er**/ as in dinner
/**oe**/ as in toe and go
/**air**/ as in pair, there, care and bear
/**ear**/ as in near, and here
/**r**/ as in write, ran

Useful common but tricky words

people looked called asked
could laughed their

STAGE 3
Growing reader: I am starting to read more words and longer
sentences with less help

Approx. 4–5 years	Oxford Levels 4 and 5	Book Bands Blue and Green

Stage 4 Gaining Confidence I sometimes read by myself, and I can read lots of everyday words

Your child will now be gaining more confidence in reading. They are likely to have reached the end of their formal phonics instruction at school, and can usually apply their phonics knowledge automatically, reading a wide range of both familiar and unfamiliar words, and recognising most common non-decodable words.

Books at Stage 4

It's useful to know what books are like at this stage so that you can help your child to choose books that you can read together.

- There is more text on the page – often 4–7 lines. Vocabulary and sentence structures are still usually quite simple and familiar, but slightly more formal language can sometimes be used.

- Words are mostly decodable but include a wide range of different spelling patterns for the same sound (e.g. 'feel', 'bead', 'shield'), and different sounds for the same spelling pattern (e.g. 'bead', 'head').

- Pictures still support the meaning of the text and sometimes help with less familiar language, but not all unfamiliar words have pictures.

- Books are becoming slightly longer and more complex, with plots sometimes worked out in more detail over more pages than before.

- Plots in stories and information in non-fiction books are becoming more detailed, so children need to think more carefully to understand and interpret them.

Read with Oxford Stage 4: *The Frog Prince and Other Tales*

Practical tips

Find a time to read with your child when they are not too tired and are happy to concentrate for about fifteen to twenty minutes, or longer if they want to.

- Don't stop sharing bedtime stories or information books with your child, even if they also like reading independently. Choose books together and enjoy talking about them.

- Try reading slightly more difficult books to your child. Hearing you read fluently will motivate them to want to read it themselves.

- Talk about the books you read. Get your child to make links between their own experience and how a character responded in the story or between their experience and relevant content in the information book.

- As well as reading books aloud together, encourage your child to read silently and independently, especially when they are re-reading favourite books.

When you come across words where there are different spelling patterns for the same sound (e.g. 'clue', 'June', 'blew'), ask your child to think of other examples.

Do the same when you find words where the same spelling pattern can be pronounced another way (e.g. 'home' and 'come').

If it's appropriate, for any new and more difficult words your child is reading, remind them to look at the letter patterns and not each individual letter. This will help them to read longer words and also to remember the spelling.

Play games to help your child become familiar with the alternative spellings for sounds.

If your child gets stuck on a word that is decodable, encourage them to say the sounds and then blend them together to make the word. Get them to read the whole sentence again. Focus on the meaning. If the word is not decodable, or is still too tricky, just read the word to your child and re-read the sentence, then move on with the text. It's the meaning that is important.

When your child re-reads a story, ask them to read it with lots of expression. Get them to use different voices for the different characters.

Talk about the story, asking your child to tell you about it, what they liked – or didn't like. Ask them if they can relate anything in the story to their own life.

When you read information books together, ask your child to tell you what they've learned, and what they found most interesting.

| STAGE 4 |
| Gaining confidence: I sometimes read by myself, and I can read lots of everyday words |

| Approx. 5–6 years | Oxford Levels 6 and 7 | Book Bands Orange and Turquoise |

Stage 5 Becoming independent I can read and enjoy a whole story by myself

Your child will be confident in their reading, and can read silently, fluently and independently most of the time. They can apply their phonics knowledge automatically, usually without sounding out, and will usually be confident in tackling unknown words using a range of strategies. They will know about different kinds of stories and different types of non-fiction, and use their experience of reading other stories to make predictions and form expectations.

Books at Stage 5

- Have at least one paragraph of text on the page – often two; occasionally there are full pages of text.

- There's a wider range of sentence structures. Vocabulary is mostly straightforward and the child will understand it even when it's not vocabulary that they would use themselves. Less familiar vocabulary may sometimes be used.

- A full range of high-frequency (sometimes called common or tricky) words are used, including a range of contractions like 'can't', 'don't', 'it's' (for 'it is').

- Pictures still support the meaning of the text, but there is less emphasis on pictures for the reading of specific words.

- Plotting and characterisation are still mostly clear and straightforward to follow, but sometimes ideas are worked out at greater length within a story. The information and discussion in non-fiction books can also be carried over more paragraphs or pages.

- Stories are often divided into short chapters so that children can read a chapter in one sitting.

Read with Oxford Stage 5:
Winnie and Wilbur: *Tidy Up, Winnie!*

Practical tips

As always, find a time to read with your child when they are not too tired and are happy to concentrate for about twenty minutes, or longer if they want to.

- Don't stop sharing bedtime stories or information books with your child, even though they also like reading independently. Choose books together and enjoy talking about them.

- Try reading a more difficult book to your child using lots of expression. This can motivate them to want to read it themselves.

- Talk about the books you and your child read together.

- Get your child to make links between their own experience and the books they are reading, whether fiction or non-fiction.

Practising reading skills

When you come across unusual words, ask your child to think of other words that mean the same thing, or other words with similar spelling patterns. This helps them to develop their vocabulary.

If your child gets stuck on a word, encourage them to break the word into syllables. Get them to re-read the whole sentence. Focus on the meaning. If they are still stuck, read the word for them, then move on.

Ask your child to read to you sometimes, using lots of expression. Ask them to use different voices for the different characters.

Talk about the story or information book, asking your child to tell you about it, and to give reasons for their opinions.

STAGE 5		
Becoming independent: I can read and enjoy a whole story by myself		
Approx. 6–7 years	Oxford Levels 8 and 9	Book Bands Purple and Gold

Stage 6 **Independent reader** I can read and understand longer chapter books by myself

Your child will read with confidence, and can read silently, fluently and independently. They can apply their phonics knowledge automatically, and use a range of strategies to read unknown words. They will know about different kinds of stories and different types of non-fiction, and can use their experience to make predictions about what they are reading. They can confidently comment on characters, story and plot, express reasoned opinions about what they read, including information books, and like to attempt longer books and books on new topics.

Books at Stage 6

- Half to three-quarters of each page is text, with some full pages of text.

- Sentences are varied, with some longer and more complicated sentences as well as shorter ones.

- Vocabulary is still mostly straightforward and the child will understand it even if it's not vocabulary that they would use themselves. Less familiar vocabulary is sometimes used.

- Pictures still help children to understand the story or information, but there isn't necessarily a picture to go with everything that happens, or for every piece of information.

- The reader finds out about characters through what they say and do, not just through descriptions. Sometimes the reader knows things that a character in the story does not.

- Storybooks are divided into chapters.

Practical tips

Keep reading with your child – find a time when they are not too tired and are happy to concentrate for about twenty to thirty minutes, or longer if they wish.

- Don't stop sharing bedtime stories or information books with your child, even though they also like reading independently.

- Offer to help your child read more difficult books, and books in different genres.

- Talk about the books you read together, and about the books you yourself are reading. Get your child to make links between their own experience and the books they are reading, whether fiction or non-fiction.

Practising reading skills

When you come across unusual words, ask your child to think of other words that mean the same thing, or other words with similar spelling patterns. This helps them to develop their vocabulary.

Encourage them to look out for unusual words in leaflets, on signs, on food packets etc., as well as in books and magazines.

If your child gets stuck on a word, encourage them to break the word into syllables. Get them to re-read the whole sentence. Focus on the meaning. If they are still stuck, read the word for them, then move on.

Ask your child to read to you sometimes, using lots of expression. Ask them to use different voices for the different characters.

Talk about the story or information book they are reading, asking your child to tell you about it, and to give you reasons for their opinions.

STAGE 6
Independent reader: I can read and understand longer chapter books by myself

Approx. 7–8 years	Oxford Levels 10, 11 and 12	Book Bands White, Lime and Brown

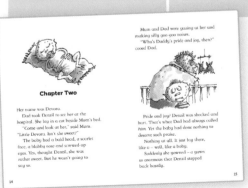

Read with Oxford Stage 6: *Disgusting Denzil*

Questions parents often ask

When should I start reading with my child?

It's never too early. Babies and toddlers enjoy looking at picture books and hearing them read aloud. Chant nursery rhymes, sing songs and share picture books from birth onwards.

Should I teach my child the alphabet?

Yes. Teach the alphabet through songs and games. Encourage your child to learn both letter names and letter sounds by playing games like 'I spy' with the letter sounds instead of the letter names. You can also use the **Read with Oxford** *Biff, Chip and Kipper: Alphabet Games* flashcards.

What if my child is more interested in the pictures than the words?

Pictures are an integral part of stories. They give important clues to what is happening. Encourage your child to look closely at the pictures while you read the story to them. Don't cover the pictures!

Ask them to make predictions about how a character is feeling by looking at their expression, or to think about what might happen next by looking at what is going on in the picture.

What if my child seems to stop making progress?

Don't worry. Children develop at different rates and they always need to consolidate what they are learning before moving on. Continue to re-read familiar books, introduce new books at the same level, play games and always be encouraging. Once they are ready, progress will resume.

What should I do if my child wants the same book over and over again?

Don't discourage them. It's good to have favourite books, and reading familiar stories will give them confidence. Introduce new stories but keep sharing old favourites too.

When and how can I first ask my child to start reading with me?

Be guided by your child – don't force the pace too early or you risk putting them off. Re-read the advice on the Stage 1 First steps (see page 9). If your child is not yet ready, spend more time reading to them and playing some of the games. If they are asking questions like *What does that word say?*, they are probably ready to begin to read. Start with a familiar story (e.g. *Goldilocks* or *The Gingerbread Man*) with lots of repeated phrases, such as *Who's been eating my porridge?* or *Run, run as fast as you can…*. Ask them to join in and place your finger under the words as you read them.

How can I support my child when they bring home books to read from school?

Once your child has started to read at school, the school will begin to send simple books home for your child to read to you. These books will most probably be in line with the phonics teaching approach used by the school. Encourage your child to read as much of each book as they can, and support them with any tricky words. In addition to books from school, you could try the traditional tales collections from **Read** with **Oxford** Stage 1, which contain simple retellings of favourite stories, written using the phonics children are learning at school. Always remember to go at your child's pace.

What is phonics?

Schools use a range of methods to teach children to read. The main one currently used to start children reading is called 'synthetic phonics'. Children are taught that the letter 's' makes a *sss* sound, as in 'sun', that we say *a* as in 'apple', and *t* as in 'tap'. Children can then start to read simple words by blending the sounds together to make a word, e.g. *s-a-t, sat*. There is more information about phonics on page 9.

What if my child makes a mistake while they're reading?

Don't stop the flow of the reading unless what they've read doesn't make sense. The meaning is the most important thing in reading in the early stages and accuracy will come.

What should I do if they get stuck on a word?

In the early stages, quietly say the word so that the flow isn't broken. As their reading develops, you can do the following:

- If it is not a tricky word, encourage them to say the sounds and then blend them together to make the word (see page 9). Read the whole sentence again. If it helps with the meaning, suggest they look at the picture.

- If it is a tricky word, or they are still stuck, simply read the word for the child so they can repeat it. Read the whole sentence again. Focus on the meaning.

What should I do if I think my child has issues with reading or might be dyslexic?

If you are concerned that your child is having issues with reading, talk to their teacher about how you can best support them.

These are some of the signs to look out for if you are concerned your child might be dyslexic: your child struggles to recognise letters and their sounds; has difficulty reading simple words without context clues; confuses or reverses words, for example *was/saw, how/who*; is frustrated because they can't keep up at school; is good at maths and other subjects but not at reading. These can be some of the indicators of dyslexia. If you are concerned, contact the British Dyslexia Association (or other national organisations) for advice, and join your local association. Look out for books and resources on dyslexia that are written for parents.

If your child complains of glare from a white page, the words moving or blurring, this may be a visual perception difficulty called Irlen Syndrome (or Scotopic Sensitivity). Consult the Irlen website for information.

Should I stop reading to my child once they've become a good reader?

No, keep reading to them and with them, for as long as they want you to. This way you can help them to access great books that they still might not be able to read for themselves. It also gives you both the continuing pleasure of sharing stories and information, just for fun.